W9-BAV-169

CANADA QUIZ

CANADA QUIZ

How Much Do You Know About Canada?

Calvin Coish

Lifestyle Books

Juv
FC61.C63 1992

Copyright © 1992 Calvin Coish

All rights reserved. No part of this publication may be reproduced or transmitted in any form or by any means without the permission of the publisher.

Lifestyle Books
6 Dawe Crescent
Grand Falls-Windsor, Nfld.
A2A 2T2
Phone (709) 489-6796

Printed and bound in Canada using recycled paper.

Canadian Cataloguing in Publication Data

Coish, E. Calvin, 1948-

Canada quiz

ISBN 0-9691126-4-5

1. Canada – Miscellanea.   I. Title

FC61.C64 1992   971'.002   C92-098661-7
F1008.3.C64 1992

QUIZ #**1**

1. Which Canadian province has the largest area?

2. He succeeded John Turner as Prime Minister of Canada.

3. What is the capital of New Brunswick?

4. What is Canada's westernmost province?

5. This Métis leader is considered the founder of Manitoba.

6. In which city would you view the Reversing Falls?

7. He brought Newfoundland into union with Canada.

8. Who wrote the children's book *Alligator Pie*?

9. How do you say "Hello" in French?

10. This animal is Canada's national emblem.

QUIZ #**2**

1. What is the capital of the Yukon?

2. Who was the first Prime Minister of Canada?

3. What is the name for an Eskimo snowhouse?

4. Who wrote the children's book *Down By Jim Long's Stage*?

5. In which city would you visit the CN Tower?

6. Vancouver Island is part of which province?

7. Who succeeded Peter Lougheed as Premier of Alberta?

8. English is one official language of Canada. What is the other?

9. What is the highest mountain in Canada?

10. This Italian explorer is credited with discovering Newfoundland around 1497 A. D.

QUIZ #<u>3</u>

1. The city of Winnipeg is located in which province?

2. One branch of the Canadian government is called the House of Commons. What is the other called?

3. Who wrote *Anne of Green Gables?*

4. This portion of mainland Canada is part of the province of Newfoundland.

5. In which Ontario city would you find the "Big Nickel"?

6. She became the first woman to lead the federal New Democratic Party.

7. The city of Calgary hosts this popular rodeo event each year.

8. What is Canada's smallest province?

9. This Canadian invented the snowmobile.

10. What is the name of the vast treeless area in Canada's north?

QUIZ #<u>4</u>

1. He became the first NDP Premier of Ontario.

2. Who wrote *The Boat Who Wouldn't Float?*

3. What is the capital of Nova Scotia?

4. This young Canadian walked halfway across Canada in 1981 to raise money for cancer research.

5. This Canadian city is the second-largest French-speaking city in the world.

6. Which ocean touches the west coast of Canada?

7. The last member of this native Newfoundland tribe died in 1829.

8. What is Canada's southernmost point?

9. What is the name of Toronto's major league baseball team?

10. In which mountain chain would you find the city of Banff?

QUIZ #<u>5</u>

1. What is Canada's easternmost province?

2. The winning team in the NHL playoffs receives this trophy.

3. This part of the U. S. Space Shuttle was designed by Canadians.

4. What is the capital of Canada?

5. This province is Canada's most densely populated.

6. Who wrote *Paper Bag Princess*?

7. What is the largest bay in Canada?

8. Who was Canada's second Prime Minister?

9. In which province would you find the community of Moose Jaw?

10. Who was Canada's first female Governor General?

QUIZ #<u>6</u>

1. What is the capital of British Columbia?

2. Which Canadian city has the largest population?

3. This female figure skater won a silver medal at the 1988 Winter Olympics.

4. These French islands are located just south of Newfoundland.

5. What does Amanda Greenleaf visit in the children's book by Ed Kavanagh?

6. Who succeeded Rita Johnston as Premier of British Columbia?

7. What is the name of Hamilton's CFL team?

8. What was the occupation of the "Group of Seven"?

9. Cape Breton Island is part of which province?

10. In what year did Canada celebrate its 100th birthday?

QUIZ #7

1. What is Canada's National Anthem?

2. In which province would you find the James Bay hydro development?

3. This Canadian Prime Minister won the Nobel Peace Prize in 1957.

4. What do the letters RCMP stand for?

5. Which country borders Canada to the south?

6. What is the capital of Saskatchewan?

7. What is the name of Vancouver's NHL team?

8. Who wrote the novel *Lunar Attractions?*

9. Which province do we associate with the Douglas Fir?

10. Which province is well-known for its potatoes?

QUIZ #8

1. In 1988 the Edmonton Oilers traded this hockey player to the Los Angeles Kings.

2. What is the longest river in Canada?

3. What symbol is in the center of the Canadian flag?

4. This Canadian singer had a hit with *Snowbird*.

5. In Newfoundland, what is a "skiff"?

6. This Ontario city has the same name as the capital of England.

7. The town of Baddeck, Nova Scotia has a museum in honour of this inventor.

8. What do the letters CBC stand for?

9. In which province would you visit Drumheller?

10. This Canadian of Ukrainian extraction succeeded Jeanne Sauvé as Governor General.

QUIZ #<u>9</u>

1. This Canadian pushed his way across Canada in a wheelchair.

2. The name Canada comes from an Indian word which means what?

3. What is the capital of Prince Edward Island?

4. The island of Newfoundland is surrounded by what ocean?

5. What is the television name of children's entertainer Ernie Coombs?

6. This member of the Group of Seven became well known for his painting *The Jack Pine*.

7. What does the French word "adieu" mean?

8. Who wrote the children's book *Jacob Two-Two Meets The Hooded Fang?*

9. What is the name of Canada's northern-most ocean?

10. What is the name of Calgary's NHL team?

QUIZ #<u>10</u>

1. This co-discoverer of insulin died in a plane crash in Newfoundland in 1941.

2. Which mineral is mined at Thetford Mines, Quebec?

3. This publication calls itself "Canada's Weekly Newsmagazine".

4. This southern Ontario city is popular with newylweds.

5. In what year was Canada born?

6. According to this singer *Life Is A Highway*.

7. In which province would you find the much-photographed community of Peggy's Cove?

8. The initials of this former Prime Minister are P. E. T.

9. What do the letters TCH stand for?

10. He defeated the NDP government and became Premier of Manitoba on April 26, 1988.

QUIZ #<u>11</u>

1. What is the name of Montreal's major league baseball team?

2. In which province would you find the city of Kamloops?

3. This Canadian actor starred in the movie *Back To The Future.*

4. What is another name for the Eskimo?

5. Who wrote the book *The Nymph and the Lamp?*

6. What is the name of the National Park on the west coast of Newfoundland?

7. This is Canada's first officially bilingual province. New Brunswick

8. In 1991 he became leader of Canada's Assembly of First Nations.

9. What is the nickname of Canada's one dollar coin?

10. Which province is the setting for *Anne of Green Gables?*

QUIZ #<u>12</u>

1. Who succeeded Douglas Campbell as Premier of Manitoba?

2. What is the name of Winnipeg's CFL team?

3. In which province would you find the city of Timmins?

4. What is Canada's largest lake?

5. This conservationist group began in Vancouver in 1970.

6. This well-known actor wrote and starred in *The Rowdyman.*

7. This large, flat area of fertile farmland includes much of Manitoba, Saskatchewan and Alberta. Praries.

8. Who was Prime Minister of Canada during "The Great Flag Debate"?

9. This British Columbia artist was well-known for her works depicting Indian lore and legends.

10. What is Canada's most northerly Inuit settlement?

QUIZ #<u>13</u>

1. This river flows into the Pacific Ocean near Vancouver.

2. The Gaspé is part of which province?

3. This trophy goes to the winning team in the CFL each year.

4. Who succeeded Joey Smallwood as Premier of Newfoundland?

5. What is the capital of Alberta?

6. This system of canals and locks links central Canada to the Atlantic Ocean.

7. This Quebec writer wrote such works as *Le Train* and *Les Belles-Soeurs*.

8. What do the letters DEW, as in DEW Line, stand for?

9. This Prime Minister was known as "The Man from Prince Albert".

10. What is the highest mountain in The Rockies?

QUIZ #<u>14</u>

1. What is the name of Montreal's NHL team?

2. In which province would you visit the town of Brandon?

3. In 1898 this naturalist, author and artist published *Wild Animals I Have Known.*

4. What was Canada's flag before the Maple Leaf design was adopted?

5. In which city would you drive across Lion's Gate Bridge?

6. Who succeeded Pierre Trudeau as Prime Minister of Canada in 1979?

7. What is the capital of Newfoundland?

8. What is Canada's most northerly island?

9. This Nova Scotia schooner is featured on the Canadian dime.

10. In which province could you attend Athabasca University?

QUIZ #<u>15</u>

1. Which Canadian province has the largest population?

2. Who succeeded James Lee as Premier of Prince Edward Island?

3. What is the name of Quebec City's NHL team?

4. A city in Ontario and towns in Nova Scotia and Newfoundland carry this name of the British royal family.

5. Canada's most famous general strike occurred in this city in 1919.

6. Where is Mount Allison University?

7. Who wrote *The Diviners?*

8. This largest living member of the deer family is found throughout Canada.

9. The McKay Bridge joins which two Maritime cities?

10. What is the capital of the Northwest Territories?

QUIZ #<u>16</u>

1. What is the name of the strait which separates Vancouver Island from the State of Washington?

2. This breed of dog is named for a Canadian province.

3. In 1959 this controversial poet won a Governor General's Award for *A Carpet for the Sun*.

4. In which province would you camp in Kejimkujik National Park?

5. What is the official flower of Ontario?

6. This dry, warm southwesterly wind often sweeps through Alberta and British Columbia in mid-winter.

7. This city had a World's Fair in 1967.

8. This Canadian wrote the first 20 *Hardy Boys* books.

9. This Ontario city was created in 1970 by the amalgamation of Fort William and Port Arthur.

10. He defeated the Social Credit government and became Premier of Alberta in August of 1971.

QUIZ #<u>17</u>

1. The Queen Charlotte Islands are part of which province?

2. Which province is well-known for its maple syrup?

3. Who lives at 24 Sussex Drive, Ottawa?

4. What is the native language of the Inuit?

5. What is the name of Toronto's CFL team?

6. This writer was 13 when he published his first book, *This Can't Be Happening At Macdonald Hall!*

7. This shaggy, horned member of the cattle family is found in Canada's Arctic.

8. In which city could you drive to the top of Signal Hill?

9. Originally known as Ile Royale, this 18th-century French colony has been restored in Nova Scotia.

10. This Canadian invented the game of basketball.

QUIZ #<u>18</u>

1. In which city could you stay at the Chateau Frontenac?

2. In which province would you climb man-made Mount Blackstrap?

3. Who succeeded Lester Pearson as Prime Minister of Canada?

4. What was Canada's first National Park?

5. Who wrote *Dance of the Happy Shades?*

6. In which province could you hike along the Bruce Trail?

7. What is the largest island in Canada?

8. This Canadian won a gold medal at the World Figure Skating Championships in 1973.

9. Who was Premier of Ontario from 1961 to 1971?

10. In which city could you study at Simon Fraser University?

QUIZ #<u>19</u>

1. This province is sometimes called "The Garden of the Gulf".

2. What is the name of Edmonton's NHL team?

3. In which part of Canada could you fish in Great Bear Lake?

4. This popular children's entertainer, born in Egypt in 1948, produced such albums as *Singable Songs for the Very Young*.

5. This city hosted the 1976 Summer Olympics.

6. He succeeded John Diefenbaker as Prime Minister of Canada.

7. What is Canada's largest native land animal?

8. In which province could you drive along the Cabot Trail?

9. The name of this river and part of Canada comes from an Indian word meaning "greatest".

10. This Canadian scientist is known for such TV programs as *The Nature of Things*.

QUIZ #<u>20</u>

1. Lake Athabasca spans which two provinces?

2. At the age of 16, she became the first person to swim across Lake Ontario.

3. This province developed from the Red River Colony.

4. What is the name of Toronto's NHL team?

5. In which city can you read the "Golden Dog" inscription?

6. Who wrote *The Incredible Canadian?*

7. This Newfoundlander invented the gas mask.

8. He became Premier of New Brunswick on June 27, 1960.

9. This singer has had such hits as *Can't Stop This Thing We Started.*

10. Which corporation is represented by the letters CPR?

QUIZ #21

1. This city hosted the 1988 Winter Olympics.

2. He became Premier of Nova Scotia on October 30, 1956.

3. This Canadian cartoonist produces the syndicated strip *For Better or for Worse*.

4. Who wrote *The Tin Flute?*

5. This Albertan was the first Canadian to scale Mount Everest.

6. In which province can you camp at Jacques Cartier Provincial Park?

7. In which city could you stand at the intersection of Portage and Main?

8. When is Canada Day?

9. This Canadian folksinger became known for such songs as *Steel Rail Blues*.

10. This speedskater won two gold medals at the 1984 Olympics in Sarajevo.

QUIZ #<u>22</u>

1. What was Edward Teach's occupation?

2. In which city can you skate on the Rideau Canal?

3. Which Strait do you cross if you take the ferry from Newfoundland to Nova Scotia?

4. This humourist has a medal named in his honour.

5. What is the name of Saskatchewan's CFL team?

6. This Canadian city is south of Detroit.

7. This Canadian rock group had a hit with *Raise A Little Hell*.

8. In which province could you climb Good Hope Mountain?

9. This NHL trophy is presented to the season's top goaltender.

10. What do the letters CTV stand for?

QUIZ #23

1. In which province would you visit Magnetic Hill?

2. What is the common name for aurora borealis?

3. In which city can you drive up Mount Royal?

4. In 1975 this poet won a Governor General's Award for *The Island Means Minago*.

5. According to Indian legend, this hairy monster lives in the mountains of British Columbia.

6. How many time zones does Canada have?

7. What is the official flower of the Yukon?

8. This Quebec-born inventor made the world's first radio broadcast.

9. In which province could you drive along the Evangeline Trail?

10. This small axe was sometimes used by North American Indians.

QUIZ #<u>24</u>

1. What do the letters V. O. N. stand for?

2. In which province could you visit Canada's Wonderland?

3. In 1962 disgruntled Canadians gave the devalued dollar this nickname.

4. Who wrote the novel *Nights Below Station Street?*

5. What are Canada's two official colours?

6. He was the first non-European to win the World Cup in downhill skiing.

7. Who succeeded Frank Moores as Premier of Newfoundland?

8. What is the official flower of Alberta?

9. Who created the ookpik?

10. What holiday is celebrated on April 23?

QUIZ #<u>25</u>

1. Which province could be called New Scotland?

2. What doughnut chain carries the name of a hockey player killed in a car accident in 1974?

3. What do the letters CUPE stand for?

4. This city has been called "Poet's Corner of Canada".

5. This Canadian missed winning the 1969 Masters golf tournament by a single shot.

6. Where is Snag?

7. Who was Canada's first native-born Prime Minister?

8. What is the name of Edmonton's CFL team?

9. He became Premier of Quebec in 1936 and again in 1944.

10. He fought Cassius Clay at Maple Leaf Gardens in 1966.

QUIZ #<u>26</u>

1. This female star of the movie *Superman* was born at Yellowknife in 1949.

2. Which province is known to the French as Terre-Neuve?

3. Who was Canada's first Governor General?

4. In which province would you find the town of Norway House?

5. Who said "The twentieth century belongs to Canada"?

6. In which city was Canada's first regular newspaper published?

7. This photographer gained fame for his superb portraits of world figures.

8. What is the longest-running play at the Charlottetown Festival?

9. This actress's real name was Gladys Mary Smith.

10. This NHL trophy is presented to the season's outstanding rookie.

QUIZ #<u>27</u>

1. She turned a limestone quarry in British Columbia into a beautiful horticultural display.

2. This province was known to natives as Abegweit.

3. This journalist profiled prominent Canadian businesses in his book *The Canadian Establishment*.

4. Orillia, Ontario, features a monument to this French explorer.

5. This political movement to promote Canada's interests was begun in 1868.

6. What is the name of the Inuit's skin-covered boat?

7. This Manitoba town has been called "The Polar Bear Capital of the World."

8. His real name was Archibald Stansfield Belaney.

9. This Canadian band leader held the world speedboat racing record in 1948.

10. In which national park could you climb Mount Edith Cavell?

QUIZ #<u>28</u>

1. What is the name of the official residence of Canada's Opposition Leader?

2. This Indian tribe were the original inhabitants of what is now Nova Scotia.

3. The Dionne Quintuplets were born in this Ontario town.

4. What is the only province without snakes, skunks or poison ivy?

5. His analysis of The Bible is titled *The Great Code*.

6. What nickname did John Diefenbaker give to the new Canadian flag in 1964?

7. Where is Old Crow?

8. Who founded the city of Ottawa?

9. What are baby beavers called?

10. Who was Canada's first female doctor?

QUIZ #29

1. Babe Ruth hit his first home run at this Canadian baseball park.

2. Who wrote the novel *Not Wanted on the Voyage?*

3. The Lady's Slipper is the official flower of which province?

4. This "one-man conglomerate" was born in New Brunswick in 1899.

5. What is the common name for Branta canadensis?

6. Which city built Canada's first domed stadium?

7. Some historians say this Irish monk visited North America around 500 A. D.

8. She won a gold medal in the giant slalom at the Winter Olympics in Innsbruck, Austria in 1976.

9. One hundred people died when a rock slide destroyed this Alberta town in 1903.

10. In which city would you stroll on the Plains of Abraham?

QUIZ #30

1. This swimmer won eight medals at the 1978 Commonwealth Games.

2. In which province could you canoe along the Miramichi?

3. It is often referred to as "Steel City".

4. This monster reportedly lives in Lake Okanagan.

5. This poet was known as "The Bard of the Yukon".

6. This Prime Minister earned the nickname "The Chief".

7. Who wrote the novel *Fifth Business?*

8. This actress was born at Penticton, B. C. in 1921.

9. If a Newfoundlander invites you to "a scoff", what will you be doing?

10. One of his paintings is called *Indians Portaging Furs.*

QUIZ #31

1. What is the name given to Canada's vast area of coniferous forests?

2. In which city would you find Queen's University?

3. This star of the Perry Mason television series was born at New Westminster, B. C. in 1917.

4. The largest non-nuclear explosion in history occurred in this city on December 6, 1917.

5. What is the name of the large body of water which separates the island of Newfoundland from the rest of Canada?

6. Who wrote the novel *Who Has Seen The Wind?*

7. He was the first Canadian to win the Boston Marathon.

8. What is the official flower of Quebec?

9. This Premier of British Columbia was born in New Brunswick in 1900.

10. In which province could you hike along the Grey Owl Trail?

QUIZ #<u>32</u>

1. This Englishman spent most of his life as a doctor and missionary in northern Newfoundland and Labrador.

2. To which province are you going if you take the ferry to Borden?

3. This Ontario bird man was born at Dover Centre, Ohio in 1865.

4. What is the official flower of British Columbia?

5. Which actor has an alter ego named Charlie Farquharson?

6. She won France's Prix Goncourt for her novel *Pélagie la-Charette*.

7. He was Canadian figure skating champion from 1971 to 1975.

8. This 1954 film starred Howard Keel, Ann Blyth and Fernando Lamas.

9. He was Premier of Saskatchewan from 1971 to 1982.

10. This island is known as "The Graveyard of the Atlantic"?

QUIZ #<u>33</u>

1. This feminist sat in the Alberta Legislature from 1921 to 1926.

2. Which Canadian city was once known as the "Gibraltar of North America"?

3. This London, Ontario native won the Miss Universe title in 1982.

4. In which province could you sail into Lunenberg harbour?

5. This trophy is presented to the most outstanding player in the Stanley Cup playoffs.

6. This New Brunswick-born actor starred in Federico Fellini's *Casanova.*

7. Who was on the English throne when Canada was born?

8. Citadel Hill with its clock tower is a landmark in which city?

9. In which province would you find the town of Penticton?

10. What is the official flower of Manitoba?

QUIZ #<u>34</u>

1. In which province could you camp in Kootenay National Park.

2. Who wrote *The National Dream?*

3. This athlete, known as Saskatoon Belle, won a gold medal for the high jump at the 1923 Olympic Games.

4. In which province would you visit the town of Wabush?

5. This city was the first capital of Upper and Lower Canada.

6. This champion race horse, born in 1961 near Toronto, has passed on its genes to many winners.

7. This economist and author of *The Affluent Society* and *The Culture of Contentment* was born in Ontario in 1908.

8. Grand Manan Island is part of which province?

9. This Canadian-born doctor formed the world's first mobile medical unit when he served with the Eight Route Army in China in 1938.

10. He was our first French Canadian Prime Minister.

QUIZ #<u>35</u>

1. Where is Wood Buffalo National Park?

2. He won the New York Film Critics Award as best supporting actor for his role in the movie *Little Big Man*.

3. What is the official flower of Saskatchewan?

4. This Canadian devised the international system of Standard Time.

5. In which city would you find Place Ville Marie?

6. *A Prairie Boy's Winter* features art by this son of Ukrainian immigrants.

7. What is the name of the Governor General's residence?

8. This Canadian soldier wrote the poem *In Flander's Fields*.

9. This Manitoba town is the largest community of people of Icelandic descent outside Iceland.

10. This Prime Minister earned the title "The Incredible Canadian".

QUIZ #<u>36</u>

1. This ship, then the world's largest, landed the first transAtlantic cable at Heart's Content, Newfoundland in 1866.

2. In 1969 this poet refused to accept a Governor General's Award for his *Selected Poems.*

3. The Soo is part of which province?

4. This star of *The Munsters* was born at Vancouver in 1922.

5. She became Lieutenant-Governor of Ontario in 1974.

6. In which province would you find Glacier National Park?

7. Who wrote the book *The Engineer of Human Souls?*

8. This hockey player was nicknamed "The Rocket".

9. This is the most northerly settlement in the world.

10. Who was Canada's first black cabinet minister?

QUIZ #<u>37</u>

1. Where is Kananaskis Country?

2. This Nova Scotian was the first person to sail solo around the earth.

3. Whose portrait is featured on the Canadian ten-dollar bill?

4. Where is Kluane National Park?

5. What was the original name of Ottawa?

6. This Canadian swimmer earned the nickname "Mighty Mouse".

7. Where is Tignish?

8. He won the 1991 Governor General's Award for his novel *Lives of the Saints.*

9. What is the name of the publication which prints Canadian Parliamentary debates?

10. This Israeli architect designed Habitat 67 featured at the Montreal World's Fair.

QUIZ #<u>38</u>

1. Where is Oka Provincial Park?

2. What is the official flower of New Brunswick?

3. Who was Canada's first native-born Governor General?

4. During the height of the Klondike Gold Rush this city had a population of 25,000.

5. He was the first jockey to ride more than 6,000 winning horses.

6. In which province could you drive the length of the Great Northern Peninsula?

7. Who wrote the novel *Close to the Sun Again?*

8. This cabinet minister in the St. Laurent Government posed the question "What's a million?"

9. Where is North Battleford?

10. One of this artist's best-known paintings features a horse running towards an oncoming train.

QUIZ #<u>39</u>

1. In which province would you visit the Republic of Madawaska?

2. Who became Premier of British Columbia in 1972?

3. This world-famous contralto was born in Montreal in 1931.

4. What does the acronym CANDU stand for?

5. What is the official flower of Nova Scotia?

6. This hockey player was nicknamed the "Golden Jet".

7. This city began as Fort Garry.

8. This novelist, born in 1885, created *The Whiteoaks of Jalna.*

9. What was the name of the 1950s Armed Forces aerobatic team?

10. Who succeeded John Robarts as Premier of Ontario?

QUIZ #<u>40</u>

1. Where is Pugwash?

2. In the 1950s she was known as Canada's "First Lady of Song".

3. It is sometimes called "The Loyalist City".

4. What do the letters CRTC stand for?

5. He became Premier of Manitoba in 1981.

6. This naturalist wrote *The Backwoods of Canada*.

7. This NHL trophy is awarded to the player who best combines skill and gentlemanly conduct.

8. Where is Red Deer?

9. This Canadian produced and directed such films as *The Cincinnati Kid* and *Fiddler on the Roof*.

10. This group of fundamentalist Christians immigrated to Saskatchewan from Russia in 1899.

QUIZ #<u>41</u>

1. This world champion rower lost only six of 350 races he took part in between 1878 and 1883.

2. Where is Grande Prairie?

3. This singer's first big hit was *Bud The Spud.*

4. This baby food was developed by three doctors in Canada.

5. Where is Riding Mountain National Park?

6. He received the first transAtlantic wireless message on Signal Hill, Newfoundland in 1901.

7. This New Brunswick clipper earned the title "Fastest Ship in the World".

8. In 1982 she received a Governor General's Award for *Home Truths: Selected Canadian Stories.*

9. In which province would you sail on Bras d'Or Lake?

10. This Canadian neurosurgeon conducted the first systematic mapping of the human brain.

QUIZ #<u>42</u>

1. He became Premier of Prince Edward Island in 1981.

2. It is sometimes called "Rose City".

3. This native of Lachine, Quebec won the Nobel Prize for Literature in 1976.

4. Jacques Cartier took this Indian chief to France, where he died.

5. This Alberta town has a UFO landing pad.

6. This Canadian-born actress starred in such films as *The Andromeda Strain* and *Atlantic City*.

7. Who was the first Canadian in space?

8. In which province would you find the town of Dauphin?

9. He was the first Canadian elected president of the United Steelworkers of America.

10. This hockey player, born in Saskatchewan in 1928, retired from the Hartford Whalers in 1980.

QUIZ #<u>43</u>

1. This famous pianist died in 1982 at the age of 50.

2. This city has been called "The Potash Capital of the World".

3. In which province would you find Galiano Island?

4. He served as Premier of Quebec from 1970 to 1976.

5. Who wrote the novel *Burden of Desire?*

6. This Canadian-born actor starred as Tonto in *The Lone Ranger.*

7. This "free" university operated in Toronto from 1968 to 1975.

8. What is the name of Montreal's CFL team?

9. He was Alberta's first Social Credit premier.

10. This Viennese-born biochemist came to Canada and became an expert on the subject of stress.

QUIZ #<u>44</u>

1. Who starred as *King of Kensington?*

2. In which city would you find Archambault Prison?

3. Where are the Torngat Mountains?

4. The Algonquin Indians believed this spirit took possession of people lost in the woods.

5. He was the first leader of the New Democratic Party.

6. What do the letters CSIS stand for?

7. This hockey player, born in Parry Sound, Ontario, won the Calder Trophy in his first year with the Boston Bruins.

8. What is Canada's largest public museum?

9. This "Mad Trapper of Rat River" was shot by the RCMP in 1932.

10. This Nova Scotian wrote *The Mountain and the Valley.*

QUIZ #<u>45</u>

1. This Canadian folksinger wrote the 1960s hit *Universal Soldier.*

2. What were the Gemini Awards originally called?

3. What is the Inuit name for a cairn of rocks built in the shape of a man?

4. This city is located about mid-way between Montreal and Quebec City.

5. This veteran *Front Page Challenge* panelist died in 1984.

6. Who was Canada's first female astronaut?

7. This Nova Scotian became Prime Minister of Canada in 1896.

8. What is the English name for the fleur-de-lis?

9. Which province has the motto "Strong and Free"?

10. In which sport did Whipper Billy Watson gain fame?

QUIZ #<u>46</u>

1. She won the 1966 Governor General's Award for *The Circle Game*.

2. How many heraldic lions appear on Canada's coat of arms?

3. This former Premier of Manitoba became Governor General of Canada in 1979.

4. In which city could you have "high tea" at the Empress Hotel?

5. You can visit a restored Viking settlement in this Newfoundland community.

6. This city is located on the Alberta-Saskatchewan border.

7. Which province has the motto "The small under the protection of the great"?

8. This Canadian won Britain's "Best Actress of the Year" award in 1978.

9. In which province could you camp in Fundy National Park?

10. In Canadian politics, what do the letters CCF stand for?

QUIZ #<u>47</u>

1. This Canadian coined the phrase "global village"?

2. What is the name for an Eskimo boot made of sealskin?

3. This writer created a character called Sam Slick?

4. This Quebec-born jockey won a record 407 horse races in 1968.

5. The Whiteshell Nuclear Research Establishment is located in which province?

6. He became Premier of Ontario in 1971.

7. Which province has the motto "Hope was restored"?

8. This Vancouver-born architect designed Simon Fraser University.

9. Where was Alberta's first oil well?

10. Who is the patron saint of Quebec?

QUIZ #<u>48</u>

1. Haida Indians are noted for carvings from this dull grey sedimentary rock.

2. He won the 1970 Governor General's Award for *The Collected Works of Billy The Kid*.

3. This chainsmoking politician founded the Parti Quebecois.

4. Where is Sioux Lookout?

5. This actor earned renown for his portrayal of Sergeant Renfrew in *Royal Canadian Air Farce*.

6. These small silvery fish roll ashore on Newfoundland beaches every summer.

7. This Canadian singer/songwriter had a hit with *Sometimes When We Touch*.

8. Whose portrait is on the Canadian five-dollar bill?

9. In which city could you visit the Peace Tower?

10. He was the first French Canadian Governor General.

QUIZ #<u>49</u>

1. This Indian Princess and poet penned *The Song My Paddle Sings.*

2. In which province could you hang your hat in Medicine Hat?

3. In 1896 this prospector and his two Indian companions discovered gold in Rabbit Creek and started the Klondike Gold Rush.

4. She won the 1956 Governor General's Award for her first novel, *The Sacrifice.*

5. The Magdalen Islands are part of which province?

6. He became Premier of Saskatchewan in 1982.

7. Which province has the motto "Loyal it began, loyal it remains"?

8. He spent 12 seasons as a quarterback with the Ottawa Roughriders, and later went on to become a high school principal.

9. Where is Shediac?

10. This singer, born in Ottawa, recorded such hits as *Diana* and *Lonely Boy.*

QUIZ #<u>50</u>

1. *Low Tide on Grand Pré* is probably the most famous poem written by this New Brunswick poet.

2. This particular landscape and vegetation is an Algonquin term meaning "grassy bog".

3. What is the name of the trophy awarded each year to Canada's best athlete?

4. He succeeded Walter Shaw as Premier of Prince Edward Island.

5. This award is the British Commonwealth's chief military decoration for bravery.

6. This community was once known as Frobisher Bay?

7. In 1973 she won the women's silver medal and, with Frank Augustyn, the prize for the best pas de deux at the Moscow International Ballet Competition.

8. Who wrote the novel *Two Solitudes?*

9. Where is Biggar?

10. Who was Prime Minister of Canada when the Constitution was brought home from Britain?

ANSWERS

QUIZ #1:

1. Quebec
2. Brian Mulroney
3. Fredericton
4. British Columbia
5. Louis Riel
6. Saint John, N. B.
7. Joey Smallwood
8. Dennis Lee
9. Bonjour
10. beaver

QUIZ #2:

1. Whitehorse
2. John A. Macdonald
3. igloo
4. Al Pittman
5. Toronto
6. British Columbia
7. Don Getty
8. French
9. Mount Logan
10. John Cabot

QUIZ #3:

1. Manitoba
2. The Senate
3. Lucy Maud Montgomery
4. Labrador
5. Sudbury
6. Audrey McLaughlin
7. Calgary Stampede
8. Prince Edward Island
9. Armand Bombardier
10. tundra

QUIZ #4:

1. Bob Rae
2. Farley Mowat
3. Halifax
4. Terry Fox
5. Montreal
6. Pacific
7. Beothucks
8. Point Pelee, Ontario
9. Blue Jays
10. Rockies

QUIZ #5:

1. Newfoundland
2. Stanley Cup
3. Canadarm
4. Ottawa
5. Prince Edward Island
6. Robert Munsch
7. Hudson Bay
8. Alexander Mackenzie
9. Saskatchewan
10. Jeanne Sauve

QUIZ #6:

1. Victoria
2. Toronto
3. Elizabeth Manley
4. St. Pierre et Miquelon
5. a distant star
6. Mike Harcourt
7. Tiger Cats
8. artists or painters
9. Nova Scotia
10. 1967

QUIZ #7:

1. O Canada
2. Quebec
3. Lester Pearson
4. Royal Canadian Mounted Police
5. United States
6. Regina
7. Canucks
8. Clark Blaise
9. British Columbia
10. Prince Edward Island

QUIZ #8:

1. Wayne Gretzky
2. Mackenzie
3. maple leaf
4. Anne Murray
5. a boat
6. London
7. Alexander Graham Bell
8. Canadian Broadcasting Corporation
9. Alberta
10. Ramon Hnatyshyn

QUIZ #9:

1. Rick Hansen
2. meeting place or village
3. Charlottetown
4. Atlantic
5. Mr. Dressup
6. Tom Thomson
7. good bye
8. Mordecai Richler
9. Arctic
10. Flames

QUIZ #10:

1. Sir Frederick Banting
2. asbestos
3. Maclean's
4. Niagara Falls
5. 1867
6. Tom Cochrane
7. Nova Scotia
8. Pierre Elliott Trudeau
9. Trans-Canada Highway
10. Gary Filmon

QUIZ #11:

1. Expos
2. British Columbia
3. Michael J. Fox
4. Inuit
5. Thomas H. Raddall
6. Gros Morne
7. New Brunswick
8. Ovide Mercredi
9. Loonie
10. Prince Edward Island

QUIZ #12:

1. Duff(erin) Roblin
2. Blue Bombers
3. Ontario
4. Lake Superior
5. Greenpeace
6. Gordon Pinsent
7. Prairies
8. Lester Pearson
9. Emily Carr
10. Grise Fiord, N. W. T.

QUIZ #13:

1. Fraser
2. Quebec
3. Grey Cup
4. Frank Moores
5. Edmonton
6. St. Lawrence Seaway
7. Michel Tremblay
8. Distant Early Warning
9. John Diefenbaker
10. Mount Robson

QUIZ #14:

1. Canadiens
2. Manitoba
3. Ernest Thompson Seton
4. the Red Ensign
5. Vancouver
6. Joe Clark
7. St. John's
8. Ellesmere Island
9. the Bluenose
10. Alberta

QUIZ #15:

1. Ontario
2. Joe Ghiz
3. Nordiques
4. Windsor
5. Winnipeg
6. Sackville, N. B.
7. Margaret Laurence
8. moose
9. Halifax and Dartmouth
10. Yellowknife

QUIZ #16:

1. Juan de Fuca
2. Newfoundland
3. Irving Layton
4. Nova Scotia
5. white trillium
6. chinook
7. Montreal
8. Leslie McFarlane
9. Thunder Bay
10. Peter Lougheed

QUIZ #17:

1. British Columbia
2. Quebec
3. The Prime Minister
4. Inuktitut
5. Argonauts
6. Gordon Korman
7. muskox
8. St. John's, Nfld.
9. Louisbourg
10. James Naismith

QUIZ #18:

1. Quebec City
2. Saskatchewan
3. Pierre Trudeau
4. Banff
5. Alice Munro
6. Ontario
7. Baffin Island
8. Karen Magnussen
9. John Robarts
10. Burnaby or Vancouver, B. C.

QUIZ #19:

1. Prince Edward Island
2. Oilers
3. Northwest Territories
4. Raffi
5. Montreal
6. Lester Pearson
7. wood bison
8. Nova Scotia
9. Yukon
10. David Suzuki

QUIZ #20:

1. Alberta and Saskatchewan
2. Marilyn Bell
3. Manitoba
4. Maple Leafs
5. Quebec City
6. Bruce Hutchison
7. Cluney MacPherson
8. Louis Robichaud
9. Bryan Adams
10. Canadian Pacific Railway

QUIZ #21:

1. Calgary
2. Robert Stanfield
3. Lynn Johnston
4. Gabrielle Roy
5. Laurie Skreslet
6. Quebec
7. Winnipeg
8. July 1
9. Gordon Lightfoot
10. Gaetan Boucher

QUIZ #22:

1. pirate
2. Ottawa
3. Cabot Strait
4. Stephen Leacock
5. Roughriders
6. Windsor, Ontario
7. Trooper
8. British Columbia
9. Vezina Trophy
10. Canadian Television Network

QUIZ #23:

1. New Brunswick
2. northern lights
3. Montreal
4. Milton Acorn
5. Sasquatch or Bigfoot
6. seven
7. fireweed
8. Reginald Aubrey Fessenden
9. Nova Scotia
10. tomahawk

QUIZ #24:

1. Victorian Order of Nurses
2. Ontario
3. Diefenbuck
4. David Adams Richards
5. red and white
6. Steve Podborski
7. Brian Peckford
8. wild or prickly rose
9. Jeannie Snowball
10. St. George's Day

QUIZ #25:

1. Nova Scotia
2. Tim Horton's
3. Canadian Union of Public Employees
4. Fredericton, New Brunswick
5. George Knudson
6. Yukon
7. Sir John Abbott
8. Eskimos
9. Maurice Duplessis
10. George Chuvalo

QUIZ #26:

1. Margot Kidder
2. Newfoundland
3. Sir Charles Stanley
4. Manitoba
5. Sir Wilfrid Laurier
6. Halifax
7. Yousuf Karsh
8. *Anne of Green Gables*
9. Mary Pickford
10. Calder Trophy

QUIZ #27:

1. Jennie Butchart
2. Prince Edward Island
3. Peter Newman
4. Samuel de Champlain
5. Canada First
6. kayak
7. Churchill
8. Grey Owl
9. Guy Lombardo
10. Jasper National Park

QUIZ #28:

1. Stornoway
2. Micmacs
3. Callander
4. Newfoundland
5. Northrop Frye
6. Pearson's Pennant
7. Yukon
8. Nicholas Sparks
9. kittens or kits
10. Emily Howard Stowe

QUIZ #29:

1. Maple Leaf Park
2. Timothy Findley
3. Prince Edward Island
4. K. C. Irving
5. Canada Goose
6. Vancouver
7. St. Brendan
8. Kathy Kreiner
9. Frank
10. Quebec City

QUIZ #30:

1. Graham Smith
2. New Brunswick
3. Hamilton, Ontario
4. Ogopogo
5. Robert W. Service
6. John Diefenbaker
7. Robertson Davies
8. Alexis Smith
9. eating
10. Cornelius Krieghoff

QUIZ #31:

1. taiga
2. Kingston, Ontario
3. Raymond Burr
4. Halifax
5. Gulf of St. Lawrence
6. W. O. Mitchell
7. Tom Longboat
8. fleur-de-lis
9. W. A. C. Bennett
10. Saskatchewan

QUIZ #32:

1. Sir Wilfred Grenfell
2. Prince Edward Island
3. Jack Miner
4. Pacific dogwood
5. Don Harron
6. Antonine Maillet
7. Toller Cranston
8. *Rose Marie*
9. Allan Blakeney
10. Sable Island

QUIZ #33:

1. Nellie McClung
2. Quebec City
3. Karen Baldwin
4. Nova Scotia
5. Conn Smythe Trophy
6. Donald Sutherland
7. Queen Victoria
8. Halifax
9. British Columbia
10. Prairie crocus

QUIZ #34:

1. British Columbia
2. Pierre Berton
3. Ethel Catherwood
4. Newfoundland
5. Kingston
6. Northern Dancer
7. John Kenneth Galbraith
8. New Brunswick
9. Norman Bethune
10. Sir Wilfrid Laurier

QUIZ #35:

1. Northwest Territories
2. Chief Dan George
3. Prairie lily or western red lily
4. Sir Sandford Fleming
5. Montreal
6. William Kurelek
7. Rideau Hall
8. John McCrae
9. Gimli
10. William Lyon Mackenzie King

QUIZ #36:

1. Great Eastern
2. Leonard Cohen
3. Ontario
4. Yvonne de Carlo
5. Pauline McGibbon
6. British Columbia
7. Josef Skvorecky
8. Maurice Richard
9. Alert, N. W. T.
10. Lincoln Alexander

QUIZ #37:
1. Alberta
2. Joshua Slocum
3. Sir John A. Macdonald
4. Yukon
5. Bytown
6. Elaine Tanner
7. Prince Edward Island
8. Nino Ricci
9. *Hansard*
10. Moshe Safdie

QUIZ #38:
1. Quebec
2. purple violet
3. Sir Vincent Massey
4. Dawson City
5. Johnny Longden
6. Newfoundland
7. Morley Callaghan
8. C. D. Howe
9. Saskatchewan
10. Alex Colville

QUIZ #39:
1. New Brunswick
2. David Barrett
3. Maureen Forrester
4. Canadian Deuterium Uranium
5. Mayflower
6. Bobby Hull
7. Winnipeg
8. Mazo de la Roche
9. Golden Hawks
10. William Davis

QUIZ #40:
1. Nova Scotia
2. Gisele MacKenzie
3. Saint John, N. B.
4. Canadian Radio-Television and Telecommunications Commission
5. Howard Pawley
6. Catherine Parr Traill
7. Lady Byng Trophy
8. Alberta
9. Norman Jewison
10. Doukhobors

QUIZ #41:
1. Ned Hanlan
2. Alberta
3. Stompin' Tom Connors
4. Pablum
5. Manitoba
6. Guglielmo Marconi
7. The Marco Polo
8. Mavis Gallant
9. Nova Scotia
10. Dr. Wilder Penfield

QUIZ #42:
1. James Lee
2. Windsor, Ontario
3. Saul Bellow
4. Donnacona
5. St. Paul
6. Kate Reid
7. Marc Garneau
8. Manitoba
9. Lynn Williams
10. Gordie Howe

QUIZ #43:

1. Glenn Gould
2. Saskatoon
3. British Columbia
4. Robert Bourassa
5. Robin MacNeil
6. Jay Silverheels
7. Rochdale
8. Alouettes
9. William "Bible Bill" Aberhart
10. Hans Selye

QUIZ #44:

1. Al Waxman
2. Montreal
3. Labrador (Newfoundland)
4. windigo
5. T. C. (Tommy) Douglas
6. Canadian Security Intelligence Service
7. Bobby Orr
8. Royal Ontario Museum
9. Albert Johnson
10. Ernest Buckler

QUIZ #45:

1. Buffy Sainte-Marie
2. ACTRA Awards
3. inukshuk
4. Trois-Rivières
5. Gordon Sinclair
6. Roberta Bondar
7. Sir Charles Tupper
8. Madonna lily
9. Alberta
10. professional wrestling

QUIZ #46:

1. Margaret Atwood
2. six
3. Edward Schreyer
4. Victoria, B. C.
5. L'Anse aux Meadows
6. Lloydminster
7. Prince Edward Island
8. Kate Nelligan
9. New Brunswick
10. Co-operative Common wealth Federation

QUIZ #47:

1. Marshall McLuhan
2. mukluk
3. T. C. Haliburton
4. Hervé Filion
5. Manitoba
6. William Davis
7. New Brunswick
8. Arthur Erickson
9. Leduc
10. St. Jean Baptiste

QUIZ #48:

1. argillite
2. Michael Ondaatje
3. René Lévesque
4. Ontario
5. Dave Broadfoot
6. caplin
7. Dan Hill
8. Sir Wilfrid Laurier
9. Ottawa
10. Georges Vanier

QUIZ #49:

1. Pauline Johnson
2. Alberta
3. George Carmack
4. Adele Wiseman
5. Quebec
6. Grant Devine
7. Ontario
8. Russ Jackson
9. New Brunswick
10. Paul Anka

QUIZ #50:

1. Bliss Carman
2. muskeg
3. Lou Marsh Trophy
4. Alexander B. Campbell
5. Victoria Cross
6. Iqaluit
7. Karen Kain
8. Hugh McLennan
9. Saskatchewan
10. Pierre Elliott Trudeau